HAL•LEONARD®

GUITAR
PLAY-ALONG

AUDIO
ACCESS
INCLUDED

PLAYBACK+
Speed • Pitch • Balance • Loop

T0039752

CONTENTS

To access audio visit:
www.halleonard.com/mylibrary

2742-0952-4413-3221

Cover photo © Photofest

ISBN 978-1-4950-0803-0

HAL•LEONARD®
CORPORATION

7777 W. BLUEMOUND RD. P.O. BOX 13819 MILWAUKEE, WI 53213

Visit Hal Leonard Online at
www.halleonard.com

Annie's Song

Words and Music by John Denver

Intro

Moderately ♩ = 148

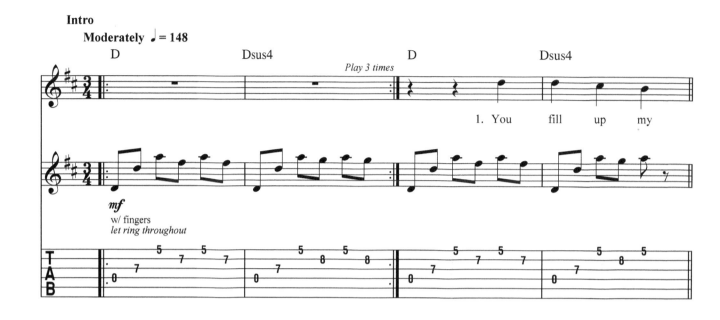

%Verse

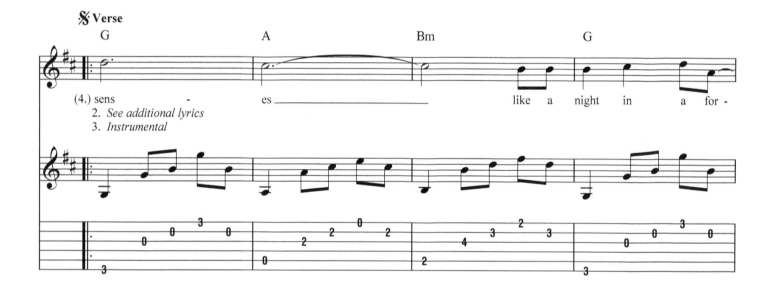

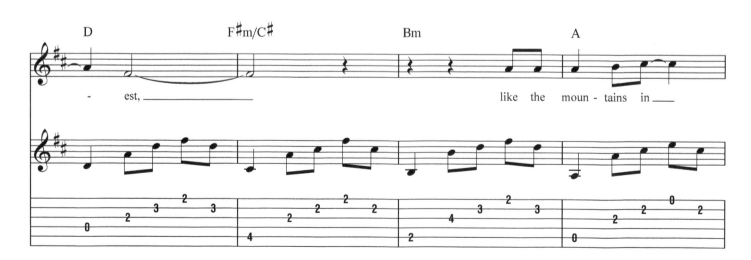

To Coda ⊕

3

Additional Lyrics

2. Come let me love you,
   Let me give my life to you,
   Let me drown in your laughter,
   Let me die in your arms,
   Let me lay down beside you,
   Let me always be with you.
   Come let me love you,
   Come love me again.

Back Home Again

Words and Music by John Denver

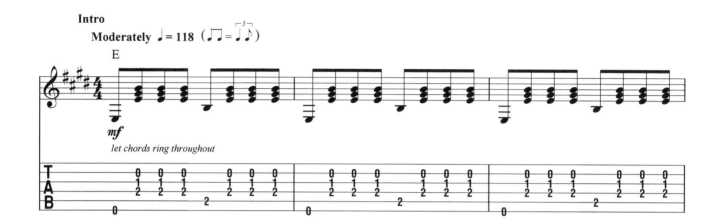

Additional Lyrics

2. He's an hour away from ridin' on your prayers up in the sky,
   And ten days on the road are barely gone.
   There's a fire softly burnin', supper's on the stove.
   But it's the light in your eyes that make him warm.

3. There's all the news to tell him, how'd you spend your time,
   And what's the latest thing the neighbors say?
   And your mother called last Friday, "Sunshine" made her cry,
   And you felt the baby move just yesterday.

4. And it's the sweetest thing I know of just spendin' time with you,
   It's the little things that make a house a home,
   Like a fire softly burnin' and supper on the stove,
   The light in your eyes that makes me warm.

Leaving on a Jet Plane

Words and Music by John Denver

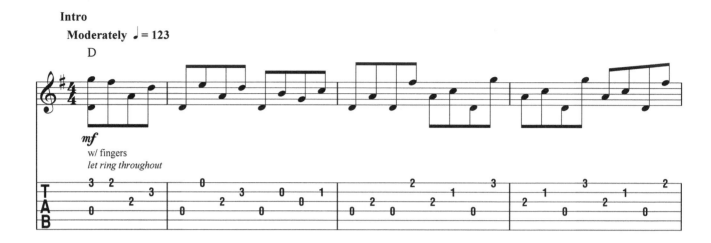

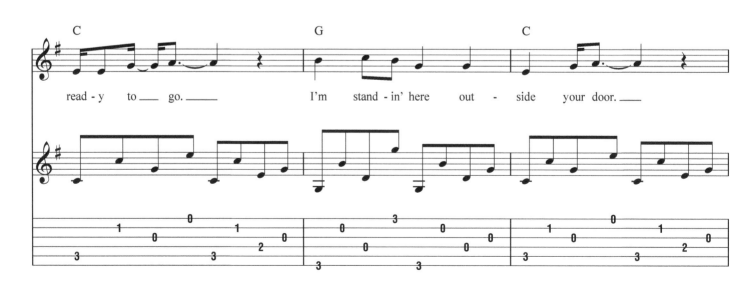

*Strum chords with index finger.

Chorus

'Cause I'm leav-in' on a jet plane, don't know when I'll be back a-gain. Oh,

To Coda

14

Additional Lyrics

2. There's so many times I let you down,
So many times I played around.
And I tell you now, they don't mean a thing.
Ev'ry place I go, I'll think of you.
Ev'ry song I sing, I'll sing for you.
When I come back, I'll bring your wedding ring.

Rocky Mountain High

Words and Music by John Denver and Mike Taylor

Drop D tuning, capo II:
(low to high) D-A-D-G-B-E

Intro
Moderately ♩ = 80

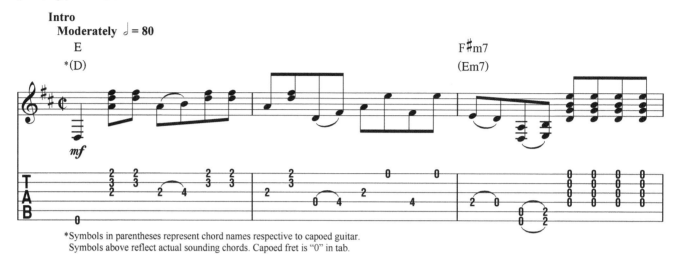

*Symbols in parentheses represent chord names respective to capoed guitar.
Symbols above reflect actual sounding chords. Capoed fret is "0" in tab.

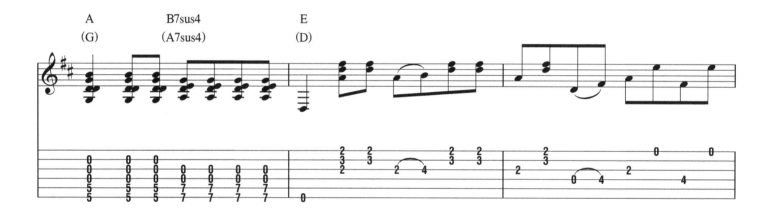

Verse

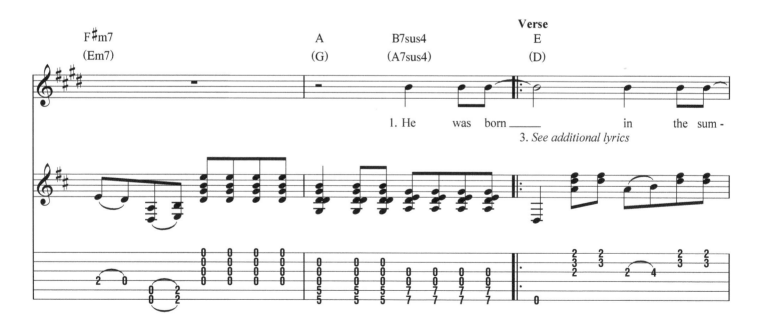

1. He was born ____ in the sum-
3. *See additional lyrics*

shad - ow from the star - light _____ is soft - er than a lull - a - by. _____

To Coda ⊕

E
(D)

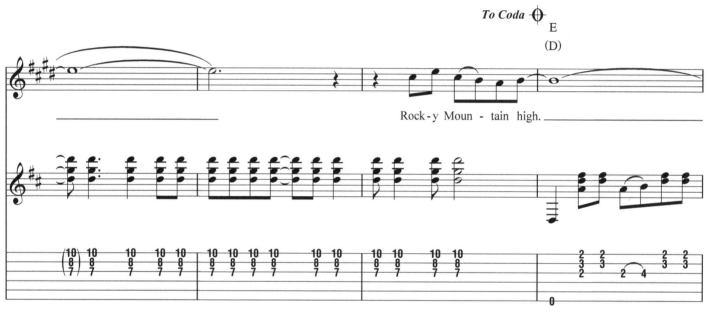

_____ Rock - y Moun - tain high. _____

F♯m7   A   B7sus4   E
(Em7)   (G) (A7sus4) (D)

_ (Col - o - rad - o. _____ Rock - y Moun - tain high. _____

High _____

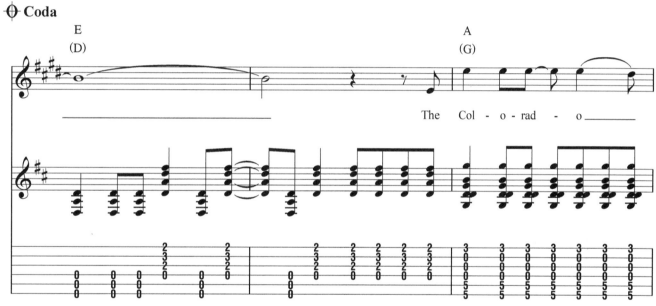

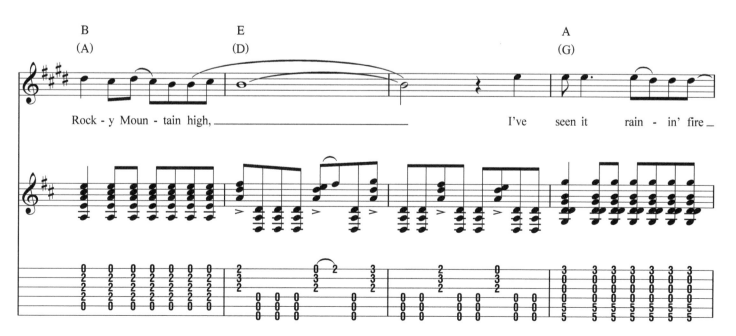

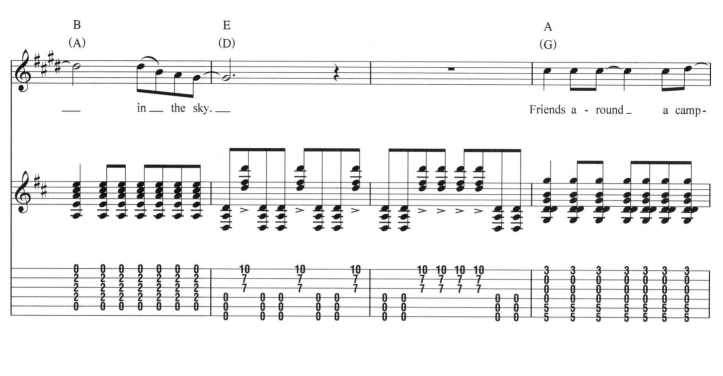

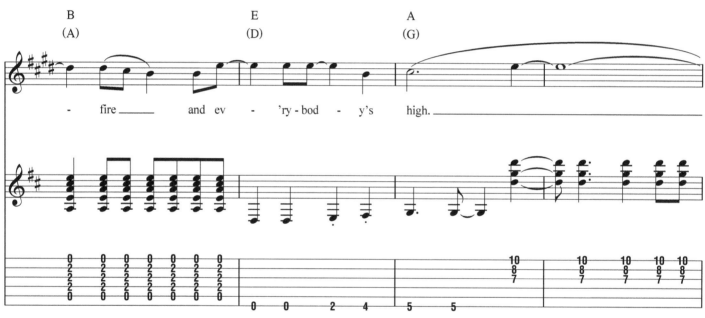

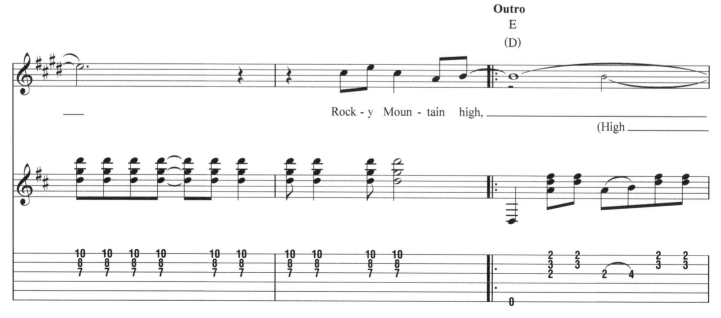

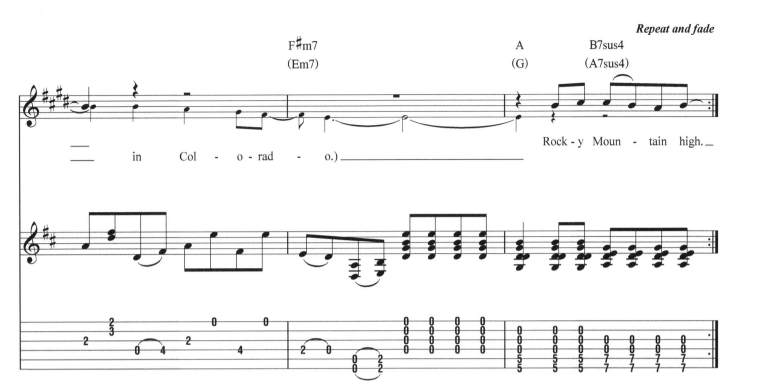

Additional Lyrics

3. He climbed Cathedral Mountains, he saw silver clouds below.
   He saw ev'rything as far as you can see.
   And they say that he got crazy once, and he tried to touch the sun.
   And he lost a friend but kept the memory.

4. Now he walks in quiet solitude, the forests and the streams.
   Seeking grace in ev'ry step he takes.
   His sight has turned inside himself to try and understand
   The serenity of a clear blue mountain lake.

Chorus 2. And the Colorado Rocky Mountain high,
   I've seen it rainin' fire in the sky.
   Talk to God and listen to the casual reply.
   Rocky Mountain high. (Colorado.)
   Rocky Mountain high. (High in Colorado.)

5. Now his life is full of wonder, but his heart still knows some fear
   Of a simple thing he cannot comprehend.
   Why they try to tear the mountains down to bring in a couple more.
   More people, more scars upon the land.

Chorus 3. And the Colorado Rocky Mountain high,
   I've seen it rainin' fire in the sky.
   I know he'd be a poorer man if he never saw an eagle fly.
   Rocky Mountain high.

Sunshine on My Shoulders

Words by John Denver
Music by John Denver, Mike Taylor and Dick Kniss

Capo III

*Symbols in parentheses represent chord names respective to capoed guitar.
Symbols above reflect actual sounding chords. Capoed fret is "0" in tab.

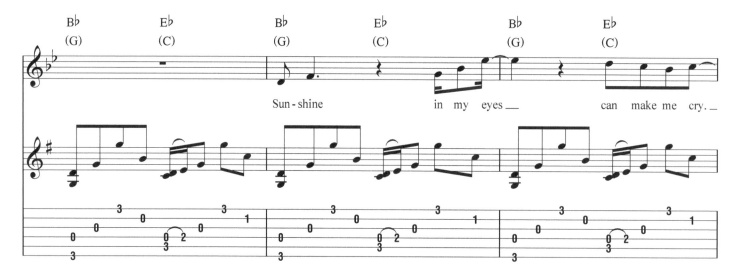

Take Me Home, Country Roads

Words and Music by John Denver, Bill Danoff and Taffy Nivert

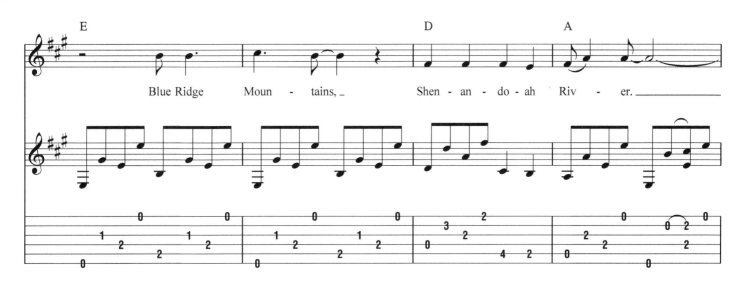

Additional Lyrics

2. All my mem'ries gather 'round her,
   Miner's lady, stranger to blue water.
   Dark and dusty, painted on the sky.
   Misty taste of moonshine, teardrop in my eye.

Thank God I'm a Country Boy

Words and Music by John Martin Sommers

Coda

Taught me how to love and how to give just a lit - tle, ___

___ and thank God I'm a coun - try boy. ___ Well, I

Outro-Chorus

got me a fine wife, I got me old fid - dle. When the sun's com - in' up I got cakes ___

___ on the grid - dle. Life ain't noth - in' but a fun - ny, fun - ny rid - dle.

Additional Lyrics

3. Well, I wouldn't trade my life for diamonds or jewels.
   I never was one of them money-hungry fools.
   I'd rather have my fiddle and my farmin' tools.
   Thank God I'm a country boy.
   Yeah, city folk drivin' in a black limousine.
   A lot of sad people thinkin', "That's a mighty keen."
   Son, let me tell you now exactly what I mean:
   I thank God I'm a country boy.

4. Well, my fiddle was my daddy's till the day he died.
   And he took me by the hand, held me close to his side.
   Said, "Live a good life, play my fiddle with pride.
   And thank God you're a country boy."
   Well, my daddy taught me young how to hunt and how to whittle.
   Taught me how to work and play a tune on the fiddle.
   Taught me how to love and how to give just a little.
   And thank God I'm a country boy. Yeah!

This Old Guitar

Words and Music by John Denver

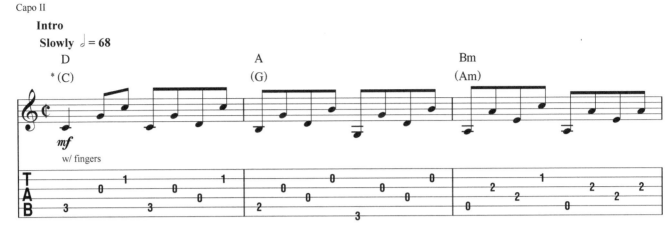

*Symbols in parentheses represent chord names respective to capoed guitar.
Symbols above reflect actual sounding chords. Capoed fret is "0" in tab.

1. This old ___ gui-tar ___ taught ___ me to sing ___
2., 3. *See additional lyrics*

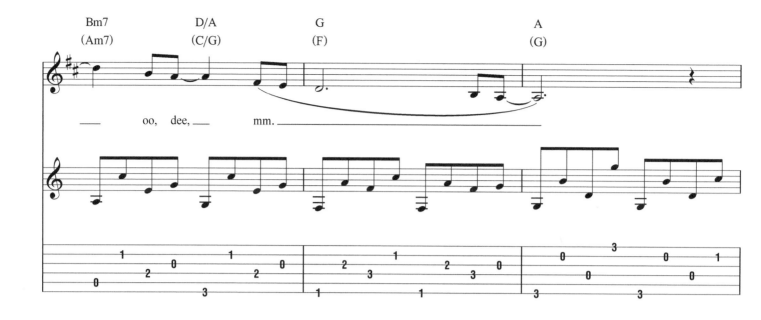

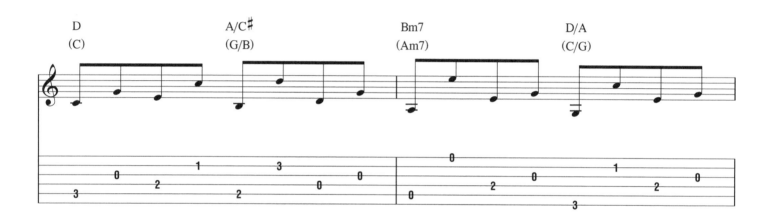

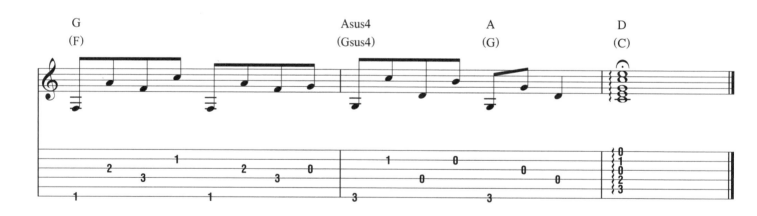

Additional Lyrics

2. This old guitar gave me my lovely lady,
   It opened up her eyes and ears to me.
   It brought us close together, and I guess it broke her heart.
   It opened up the space for us to be.
   What a lovely place and a lovely space to be.

3. This old guitar gave me my life, my living,
   All the things you know I love to do.
   To serenade the stars that shine from a sunny mountainside,
   And most of all to sing my songs for you.
   I love to sing my songs for you.